ALI ON ALI

Why He Said What He Said
When He Said It

HANA ALI

with Danny Peary

WORKMAN PUBLISHING • NEW YORK

Library of Congress Cataloging-in-Publication Data is available.

ISBN 978-1-5235-0346-9

Design by Jean-Marc Troadec
Photo research by Kenneth Yu
Editing by Danny Cooper
Production editing by Amanda Hong
Production management by Steven Bucsok
Research by Carol Summers
Photos credits appear on page 156.

Workman books are available at special discounts when purchased in bulk for premiums and sales promotions as well as for fund-raising or educational use. Special editions or book excerpts also can be created to specification. For details, contact the Special Sales Director at the address below, or send an email to specialmarkets@workman.com.

Workman Publishing Co., Inc.
225 Varick Street
New York, NY 10014-4381
workman.com

WORKMAN is a registered trademark of Workman Publishing Co., Inc.

Printed in the United States of America
First printing March 2018

10 9 8 7 6 5 4 3 2 1

This book is dedicated
to all of my father's fans.
He loved you as much as you
love him. You were the
wind beneath his wings.

Dad and me, 2004

INTRODUCTION

There are many reasons my father, Muhammad Ali, had the most recognized face in the world, was the athlete most written about, and is arguably the greatest athlete of all time.

Dad would have told you that it was because he lived the life of a hundred men. He was an Olympic gold medalist, a three-time world heavyweight champion, a conscientious objector, a Messenger of Peace, a hostage negotiator, and a loving father. He ignited the Olympic cauldron and received the Presidential Medal of Freedom. Now loved and admired for the same reasons he was once despised and scorned, Muhammad Ali was a living legend.

My father once said, "I've been an actor my entire life. I wrote my own lines. I directed my own scenes. I starred in my own plays. I sold my own legend." Another wise man once said, "Life itself is a quotation." Within these pages is a colorful mix of my father's humorous, poignant, inspirational, political, and philosophical quotes. I have given the explanations behind each of them, but this book would not be what it is without the hard work and dedication of sportswriter Danny Peary, who helped me gather the quotes herein and research their origins.

Together we give you *Ali on Ali*.

While my father is no longer of this world, the echo of his most famous ringside shout, "I am the greatest!" will live on, reminding us and generations to come what he hoped it would: Impossible is nothing when we love and believe in ourselves. I hope that you will be both moved and amused by what you read, and that this collection of my father's enduring words, thoughts, and ideas will give new insight to those who knew him and followed his remarkable boxing career. And that it will inspire generations learning about him for the first time to further study his incredible legacy.

In my eyes, he was and always will be the Eighth Wonder of the World.

— HANA YASMEEN ALI

"When will they ever have another fighter who writes poems, predicts rounds, beats everybody, makes people laugh, makes people cry, and is as tall and extra-pretty as me? **IN THE HISTORY OF THE WORLD FROM THE BEGINNING OF TIME, THERE'S NEVER BEEN ANOTHER FIGHTER LIKE ME.**"

My father reflected on his impact on boxing history to Thomas Hauser for his 1991 biography, *Muhammad Ali: His Life and Times*. Whatever the future holds, he's already been proven correct.

"It's a funny feeling to look down on the world and know that EVERY PERSON KNOWS ME."

My father spoke about being the most famous person on the planet to Chicago journalist Bob Greene as he looked out the window during a flight from the Windy City to Washington, DC. Greene would use this quote in the profile he was writing for the December 1983 issue of *Esquire* magazine, which was titled "Muhammad Ali Is the Most Famous Man in the World." My father was always amazed at how famous he had become. He used his fame for good and always enjoyed being Muhammad Ali.

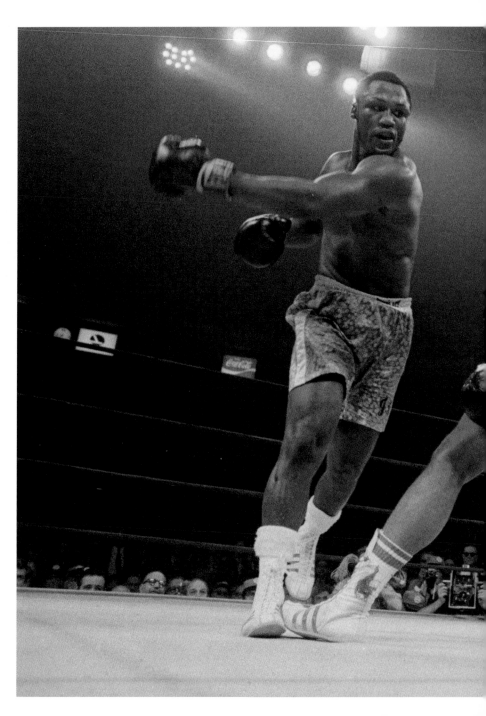

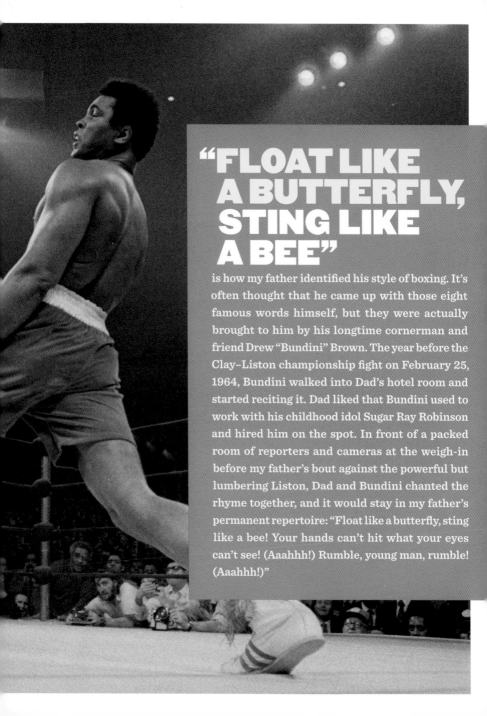

"FLOAT LIKE A BUTTERFLY, STING LIKE A BEE"

is how my father identified his style of boxing. It's often thought that he came up with those eight famous words himself, but they were actually brought to him by his longtime cornerman and friend Drew "Bundini" Brown. The year before the Clay–Liston championship fight on February 25, 1964, Bundini walked into Dad's hotel room and started reciting it. Dad liked that Bundini used to work with his childhood idol Sugar Ray Robinson and hired him on the spot. In front of a packed room of reporters and cameras at the weigh-in before my father's bout against the powerful but lumbering Liston, Dad and Bundini chanted the rhyme together, and it would stay in my father's permanent repertoire: "Float like a butterfly, sting like a bee! Your hands can't hit what your eyes can't see! (Aaahhh!) Rumble, young man, rumble! (Aaahhh!)"

"Every man wants to believe in himself. And every man wants to be fearless. WE BECOME HEROES WHEN WE STAND UP FOR WHAT WE BELIEVE IN."

These are powerful words from my father. The familiar final sentence has been cited as a stand-alone quote for decades, but these three sentences weren't strung together until we coauthored *The Soul of a Butterfly* in 2004. Looking back to a time *before* he proved himself to be a hero in the public eye, he wrote a fourth line that deserves to be just as well-known:

"I was just a kid from Kentucky who had the faith to believe in himself and the courage TO FOLLOW HIS HEART."

One day I asked my father how he found the strength to do all that he did. His reply was enlightening to me and the world:

"Service to others is the rent we pay for our room in heaven."

These words are attributed to Wilfred Grenfell, a nineteenth-century British medical missionary, but my father made them his own.

Dad with the twins Jamillah and Rasheda, Maryum, Mohammad Jr., and me on his lap, 1976

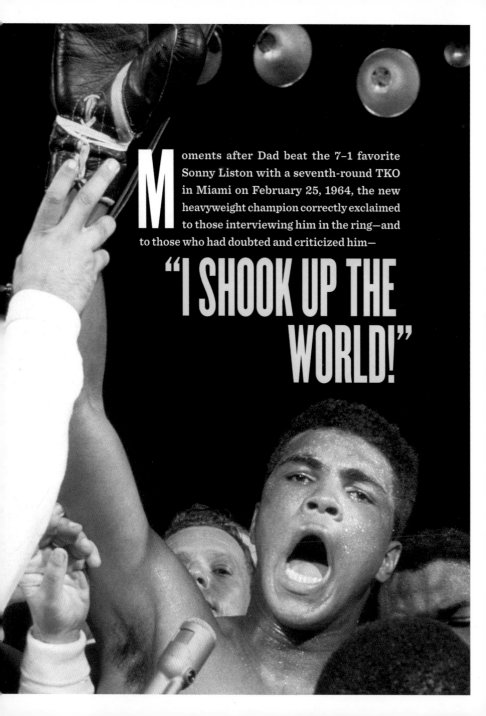

Moments after Dad beat the 7–1 favorite Sonny Liston with a seventh-round TKO in Miami on February 25, 1964, the new heavyweight champion correctly exclaimed to those interviewing him in the ring—and to those who had doubted and criticized him—

"I SHOOK UP THE WORLD!"

"I AM THE GREATEST!"

At 19, when my father was still known as Cassius Clay, he went on a local radio show in Las Vegas to promote his June 26, 1961, fight with Hawaiian boxer Duke Sabedong. Another guest was 46-year-old superstar wrestler George Wagner, aka Gorgeous George, who became wrestling's best-known villain by constantly bragging about his good looks. My father went to one of his wrestling matches and saw an arena full of fans who'd paid good money just to see the loudmouth Gorgeous George lose. Dad had been insisting he was "The Greatest" boxer at post-Olympics parades, but now his boasts had a new purpose—to attract hordes of fans who wanted his opponents to shut him up. Over his career, he never stopped bragging and being outrageous. Whether he was seen as a villain or hero to boxing fans, "The Greatest" became his permanent sobriquet and his ultimate expression of Black Pride.

When my father announced that he was a member of the Nation of Islam on February 26, 1964, he temporarily called himself Cassius X. He soon took the Muslim name Muhammad Ali, given to him by his spiritual mentor, Elijah Muhammad, who defined Muhammad as "one worthy of all praises" and Ali as "the most high." This quote was his explanation to Daniela Morera for the August 1977 issue of *Interview*:

"**CASSIUS CLAY** is a name that white people gave to my slave master. Now that I am free, that I don't belong anymore to anyone, that I'm not a slave anymore, I gave back their white name, and I chose a beautiful African one."

"IT'LL BE A KILLA, A CHILLA, A THRILLA, WHEN I GET THE GORILLA IN MANILA."

A s he good-naturedly punched a small rubber gorilla that was meant to represent Joe Frazier, my father, the world champion for a second time, used this catchy phrase to help promote his upcoming third fight with the former champion in the Philippines on October 1, 1975. Dad would win two out of three bouts of their legendary rivalry, and he said that Frazier brought out the best in him.

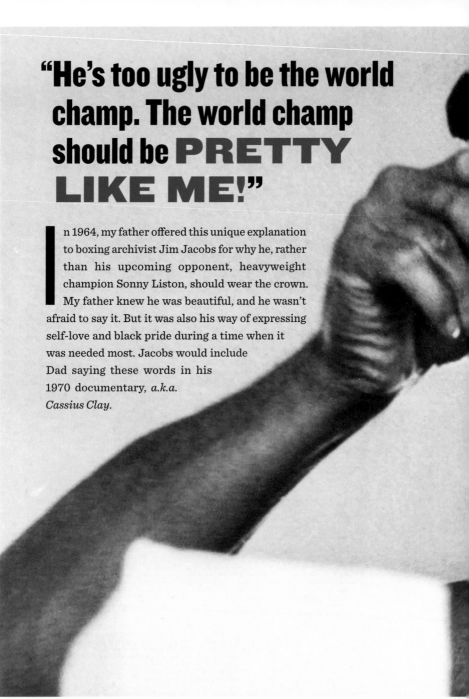

"He's too ugly to be the world champ. The world champ should be PRETTY LIKE ME!"

I n 1964, my father offered this unique explanation to boxing archivist Jim Jacobs for why he, rather than his upcoming opponent, heavyweight champion Sonny Liston, should wear the crown. My father knew he was beautiful, and he wasn't afraid to say it. But it was also his way of expressing self-love and black pride during a time when it was needed most. Jacobs would include Dad saying these words in his 1970 documentary, *a.k.a. Cassius Clay.*

"YOU SO UGLY,

you have to sneak up on the mirror so it won't run off the wall."

This was one of my father's zingers meant to rattle heavyweight champion Sonny Liston so that once their title match started, he'd be so angry he'd forget how to fight.

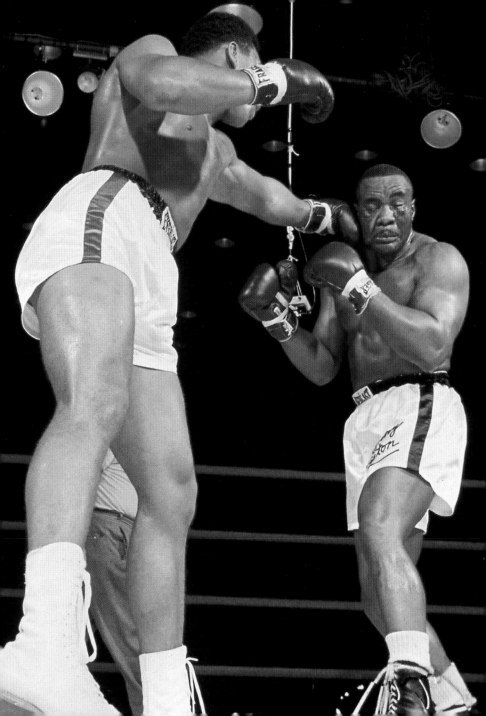

"I AIN'T GOT NO QUARREL WITH THEM VIETCONG."

My father was heavily criticized by the political establishment and the mainstream media for refusing induction into the armed forces. He indicted the American war effort in Vietnam as racist oppression against a poor, dark-skinned population and for sending African Americans to fight its war when there were still places in their own country where they couldn't eat or use the restroom. He condemned the government for not tolerating his conversion to Islam and for refusing to recognize his stance as a conscientious objector on religious grounds. On February 17, 1966, he learned that his draft status had been changed from 1-Y to 1-A, making him draft eligible. When reporters called him in Miami to ask if he'd be willing to fight in the controversial war, he gave this famous statement, resulting in nationwide headlines, and overnight it made him a hero to those in the antiwar movement.

Speaking to reporters in 1966, he further explained his views on the war:

"My conscience won't let me go shoot my brother, or some darker people, or some poor hungry people in the mud for big powerful America. And shoot them for what? They never called me nigger, they never lynched me, they didn't put no dogs on me, they didn't rob me of my nationality, rape and kill my mother and father. . . . Shoot them for what? . . . HOW CAN I SHOOT THEM POOR PEOPLE? . . . JUST TAKE ME TO JAIL."

My father didn't believe in killing other human beings "unless it's a holy war declared by God himself." He didn't believe he should fight in an unjust war when there were restaurants in America he still couldn't eat in. He said that if fighting would free his people, he wouldn't have to be drafted—he'd enlist the next day. But his real enemy and oppressor was racism in America. The military offered him deals and promised him that he'd never see the battlefield and would do boxing exhibitions, like Joe Louis did in World War II. But he wasn't like Joe Louis. As he said, he was free to be who he wanted to be.

"Once Muhammad came on the scene, all of us had to become something different than just some athlete. He was like a Porsche, maybe even a total eclipse. Something you just don't see—a phenomenon."

—GEORGE FOREMAN

"**Muhammad Ali was a god, an idol, and an icon. He was boxing. Any kid that had the opportunity to talk to Ali, to get advice from Muhammad Ali, was privileged. He's always given me time to ask questions, although I was so in awe that I didn't ask questions.**"

—SUGAR RAY LEONARD

"I CAME TO LOVE ALI. I CAME TO SEE THAT I WAS A FIGHTER AND HE WAS HISTORY."

—FLOYD PATTERSON

"If you treated Ali right, he'd treat you right. And if you didn't treat him right, he'd still treat you right. That's just one reason why people love Ali."

—LARRY HOLMES

"I AM THE KING OF THE WORLD!"

My father joyfully shouted these words while running around the ring after Sonny Liston refused to get off his stool for the seventh round in their February 25, 1964, title fight. Five weeks after his twenty-second birthday he was the new world heavyweight boxing champion.

"My greatest accomplishments in life were achieved outside the ring, and my greatest privilege in life was becoming a messenger of peace and love."

My father was thankful that he was able to use his fame to help promote his religion and spread its true meaning. Dad and I included this quote, which reveals how he was perceived by people around the world, in our 2004 book, *The Soul of a Butterfly.*

Mom (Veronica Porché), Dad, and me, 1976

My father, a young Cassius Clay, was feeling patriotic after winning the light-heavyweight boxing gold medal at the 1960 Olympics in Rome by beating Polish three-time European champion Zbigniew Pietrzykowski. So when he stepped off the plane at Standiford Field Airport upon his return to Louisville, he recited his new poem, "How Cassius Took Rome," which begins:

"To make America the greatest is my goal,
So I beat the Russians, and I beat the Pole,
and for the USA won the Medal of Gold.
Italians said, 'You're greater than the Cassius of old.'"

"I had to prove you could be a new kind of black man. I had to show that to the world."

When interviewed at his home in Michigan for the 1998 biography *King of the World: Muhammad Ali and the Rise of an American Hero*, my father told author David Remnick that he wanted his image to be entirely different from those of the previous two African American heavyweight champions: the illiterate, menacing Sonny Liston and the humble and conservative Floyd Patterson.

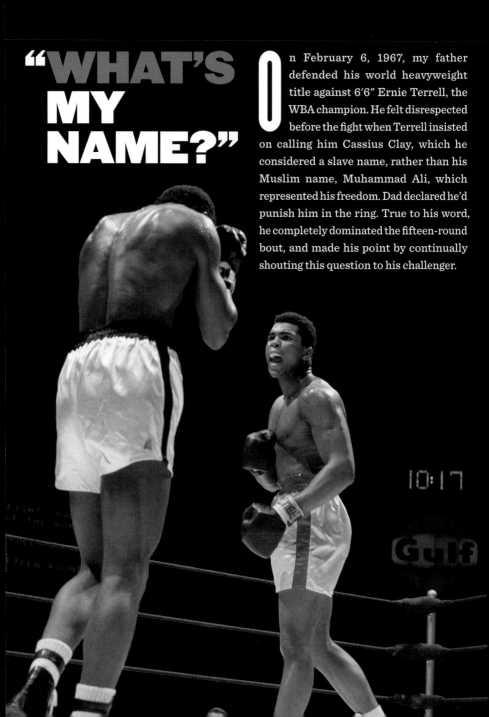

"WHAT'S MY NAME?"

On February 6, 1967, my father defended his world heavyweight title against 6'6" Ernie Terrell, the WBA champion. He felt disrespected before the fight when Terrell insisted on calling him Cassius Clay, which he considered a slave name, rather than his Muslim name, Muhammad Ali, which represented his freedom. Dad declared he'd punish him in the ring. True to his word, he completely dominated the fifteen-round bout, and made his point by continually shouting this question to his challenger.

In the mid-1960s, my father was riding in the backseat of a New York City taxi when a reporter pulled up beside him and boldly asked what he'd do if he weren't a boxer. He replied,

"I'd have been the world's greatest at whatever I did. If I were a garbageman, I'd be the world's greatest garbageman! I'd pick up more garbage and faster than anyone has ever seen."

Dad promoting the film The Greatest, *1977*

"This kid fights great. He's got speed and endurance. But if you sign to fight him, INCREASE YOUR INSURANCE."

During his pursuit of Sonny Liston's heavyweight crown in 1963 and early 1964, my father wrote humorous poems about who he was and how he would take down Liston. Most notably, the title track of his record *I Am the Greatest!* contained this and other funny verses that Dad loved to recite over the years:

"This is the legend of Cassius Clay,
The most beautiful fighter in the world today.
He talks a great deal, and brags indeed-y,
Of a muscular punch that's incredibly speedy."

"Here I predict Mr. Liston's dismemberment
I'll hit him so hard, he'll wonder where
October and November went."

"When Cassius says a mouse can outrun
a horse, don't ask how—put your money
where your mouse is."

"What's wrong with me going to jail for something I believe in? Boys are dying in Vietnam for something they don't believe."

My father was at peace with the possibility of a five-year prison term for refusing to be inducted into the army. He gave his explanation for this when interviewed for the June 1970 issue of *Black Scholar*. Fortunately, the United States Supreme Court granted his appeal in 1971.

asked Dad why he kept the people that he knew had stolen from him in his life. After a long pause, he said three wise things that I would place in my 2000 book, *More Than a Hero*, under the heading "The Lesson":

"We all have committed sins—some big, some small. In the end, we all ask God for forgiveness. If God forgives, we too should forgive. Everyone deserves a second chance."

"Everyone is trying to live the best they can with the hand that they've been dealt. It's not always easy. Life is not equally kind to us all."

"Remember to treat everyone with respect and equality, and God will always bless you."

My father wasn't bitter about having contracted Parkinson's disease. He saw it as a way to connect to people as he couldn't when he was a champion boxer in top physical condition. In 1988, he said,

"They thought I was Superman. Now they can say, 'He's human like us.'"

Me with Dad at his training camp, Fighter's Heaven, 1977

As a true Muslim, my father was always thinking about the afterlife. He believed every day is Judgment Day and it was up to him to save his own soul. He told biographer Thomas Hauser,

"**Every night when I go to bed, I ask myself, 'If God were to judge me just on what I did today, would I go to heaven or hell?'**"

"I didn't know how, but I knew that I was going to help my people. Somehow, I WAS GOING TO MAKE A DIFFERENCE IN THE WORLD."

Whether he was in a mosque, a college lecture hall, or at home with us kids, my dad spoke often about how everyone must have a purpose in life. Although he hadn't articulated it yet, he felt he had a purpose even as a boy, as he revealed to Thomas Hauser for his 1991 biography, *Muhammad Ali: His Life and Times*. He explained his calling:

"Some people have special resources inside, and when God blesses you to have more than others, you have a responsibility to use it right."

"Ali was by far the most interesting athlete of my generation. Some guys came close: Bill Russell, Joe Namath, Willie Mays. But Ali was electrifying when he was at his best and champion. He towered above everybody else."

—GEORGE PLIMPTON

"He is America's Greatest Ego. He is also . . . the swiftest embodiment of human intelligence we have had yet, he is the very spirit of the twentieth century, he is the prince of mass man and the media."

—NORMAN MAILER

"If people from outer space came to Earth and we had to give them one representative of our species to show them our physical powers, our spirituality, our decency, our warmth, our kindness, our humor, and most of all our capacity to love—it would be Ali."

—DICK GREGORY

"Too many people go to their grave with their music still inside them. Muhammad Ali lived the gift of life to the fullest."

—THOMAS HAUSER

My dad wasn't the first guest on television talk shows to joke with the hosts about small appearance fees, but to such varied hosts as Joe Namath in 1969, Dinah Shore in the 1970s, Britain's Michael Parkinson in 1971, and Joanna Lumley in 1989, he did it in rhyme:

"I LOVE YOUR SHOW, AND I LIKE YOUR STYLE, BUT YOUR PAY IS SO CHEAP I WON'T BE BACK FOR A WHILE."

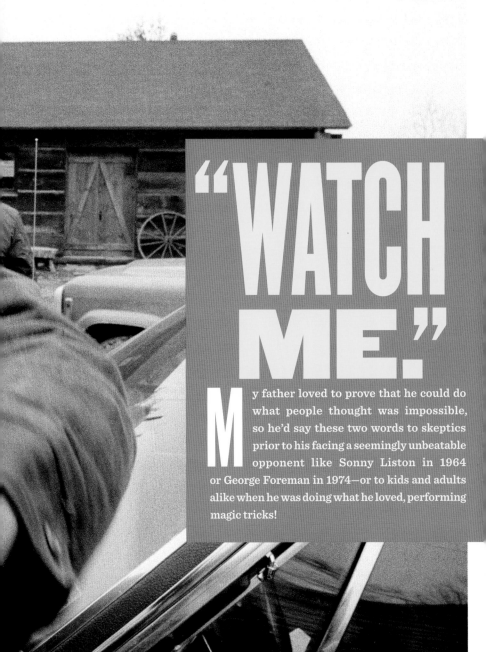

"WATCH ME."

My father loved to prove that he could do what people thought was impossible, so he'd say these two words to skeptics prior to his facing a seemingly unbeatable opponent like Sonny Liston in 1964 or George Foreman in 1974—or to kids and adults alike when he was doing what he loved, performing magic tricks!

My father and Martin Luther King Jr. had different religious beliefs, but they were both against the war in Vietnam and admired each other for their civil rights activism. When they both appeared at a rally for fair housing in Louisville, Kentucky, on May 10, 1967, Dad told him,

"In your struggle for freedom, justice, and equality, I AM WITH YOU."

"The man who views the world at fifty the same as he did when he was twenty has wasted thirty years of his life."

British interviewer David Frost said my father gave him a card with this inscription in 1974. It was one of Dad's favorite quotes.

"IF I FIND THE KID WHO STOLE MY BIKE, I'LL WHUP HIM."

This first documented quote by my father was made when he was 12 years old. After his cherished new Schwinn bike was stolen in 1954, he said this tearfully to policeman Joe Martin, who happened to be a boxing trainer. Martin told my father that before he fought anyone, he'd better learn how to box—then he offered to give Dad lessons at the Columbia Gym in Louisville. My father never found the bicycle thief, but he discovered his life's purpose. Dad trained with Joe Martin for years and boxed on his local TV show, *Tomorrow's Champions*. But he always said that it was a black man named Fred Stoner, with whom he trained in secret at Grace Community Center, who taught him the true science of boxing.

"BETTER FAR FROM ALL I SEE/ TO DIE FIGHTING TO BE FREE/ WHAT MORE FITTING END COULD BE?"

Prior to a 1972 fight with Al "Blue" Lewis in Dublin, my father was interviewed on Irish television. He recited these opening words from his poem written from the perspective of an African American inmate during the four-day Attica Prison uprising in upstate New York in September 1971, resulting in more than 40 deaths of inmates, guards, and civilians.

"I just wish people would love everybody else the way that they love me. It would be a better world."

My father said these sincere words as part of a speech he gave at colleges and universities during his exile from boxing in the late 1960s.

I once asked my father if he'd rather be the smartest man in the world with a little heart or a man of common knowledge who had a heart of gold. He told me,

"The man with all the knowledge, but with the little heart, he can only get so far. THE MAN WITH ALL THE LOVE AWAITS THE OPEN DOORS OF HEAVEN."

Celebrating my first birthday, 1977

"I don't have to be what you want me to be.

I'M FREE TO BE WHAT I WANT TO BE."

Dad said this famous quote on February 26, 1964, the morning after he defeated Sonny Liston and became the world heavyweight champion. Before hundreds of reporters at a press conference at the Convention Hall in Miami, my father was responding to a hostile journalist who pressed him on whether he was a "card-carrying" member of the "Black Muslims." This quote reflected who he was, so over the years he'd repeat it many times and in various contexts. For instance, overseas, he'd tell African and Indian students, **"I'd give up everything for what I believe. I'm a free man. I don't belong to nobody."**

"IF YOU EVEN DREAM OF BEATING ME, YOU'D BETTER WAKE UP AND APOLOGIZE."

T his was one of Dad's favorite lines. It always got a laugh, so over the years, he'd include it in his litany of quick boasts on talk shows. The quote evolved from "If he dreamed he did, he'd apologize," which is how my father responded to Howard Cosell when asked if Sonny Liston could come up with a way to neutralize his footwork in their upcoming May 25, 1965, rematch. Even before that, when discussing contender Cleveland Williams to Alex Haley for the October 1964 issue of *Playboy*, he said, "If he even *dreamed* he fought me, he'd apologize."

"IT BECAME MY MISSION TO SHOW HIM THE ERROR OF HIS FOOLISH PRIDE. BEAT IT INTO HIM."

"Do not forget that we needed each other to produce some of the greatest fights of all time."

"IF WE WERE TWINS IN THE BELLY OF OUR MAMA, I'D REACH OVER AND STRANGLE HIM."

—JOE FRAZIER

"I THINK HE SHOULD BE LOCKED UP FOR IMPERSONATING A FIGHTER."

—SONNY LISTON

"WHEN YOU COME TO THE FIGHT, DON'T BLOCK THE AISLE AND DON'T BLOCK THE DOOR. YOU ALL WILL GO HOME AFTER ROUND FOUR."

Dad correctly predicted his victory over the once-great but aged Archie Moore by TKO in the fourth round on November 15, 1962, in Los Angeles.

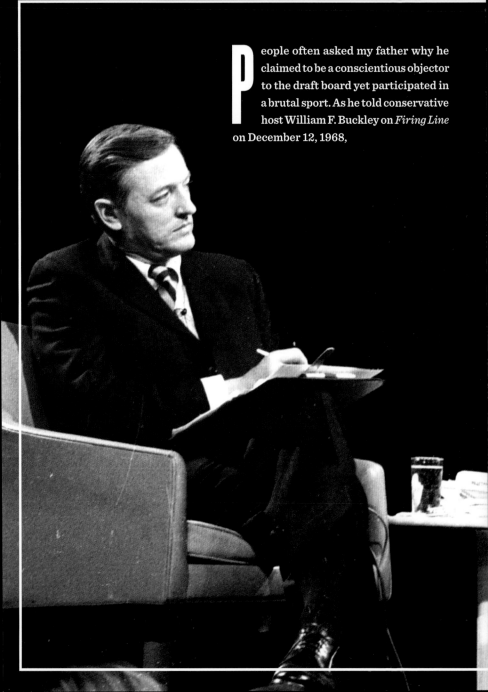

People often asked my father why he claimed to be a conscientious objector to the draft board yet participated in a brutal sport. As he told conservative host William F. Buckley on *Firing Line* on December 12, 1968,

"**BOXING** CAN'T BE COMPARED TO **WAR.**"

When Dad went to England to fight Henry Cooper on June 18, 1963, he stepped into the ring wearing a huge jeweled crown and a fancy robe with letters on the back that read "Cassius the Great." Some disgruntled fans booed and even threw things. He explained his bold adornment to reporters after winning the match:

"I understand you have a queen of England, BUT YOU DON'T HAVE A KING."

"I never thought of losing, but now that it's happened, the only thing is to do it right. That's my obligation to all the people who believe in me. We all have to take defeats in life."

My father didn't like to lose but was always gracious and philosophical about it. His second professional loss was a shocking twelve-round split decision to underdog Ken Norton at the Sports Arena in San Diego on March 31, 1973. He won the rematch in September of that year, and again in a world title defense in 1976. Dad had great respect for Norton and was the third person to the hospital when Ken endured a near-fatal car accident in 1986. He was touched by my father's concern, and they spent a couple of Thanksgivings together over the years. His daughter, Kenisha, and I are best friends.

"MY WAY OF JOKING IS TO TELL THE TRUTH. That's the funniest joke in the world."

My father said this often, but it's actually a rewording of what he first heard as a boy from his mother, Odessa, whom he called Mama Bird. My grandmother always said, "I'm going to tell the truth! It pays to tell the truth."

"The only religion that matters is the real religion—love."

D ad was quoted as saying this by his friend and biographer Davis Miller in his article "I'm More Human Now," in the *Detroit News* on January 17, 1997.

Me and Dad at Fighter's Heaven, 1977

"Hating people because of their color is wrong. And it doesn't matter which color does the hating. It's just plain wrong."

M y father expressed what he learned as a child in his 1975 autobiography, *The Greatest: My Own Story.*

"I studied life, I studied people, and I'm educated on this, but when it comes to reading and writing, I'm not—I may be illiterate in that. But when it comes to common sense, when it comes to feelings, when it comes to love, compassion for people, then I'm rich."

M y father said this on December 7, 1974, at the Mayfair Hotel in London, during his third conversation with Michael Parkinson on his popular BBC talk show. Parkinson's four sit-downs with my father are my all-time favorite interviews of him.

n 1964, my father was training at the 5th Street Gym in Miami for his first fight with Sonny Liston when the Beatles, in town for their second appearance on *The Ed Sullivan Show*, stopped by to meet the young contender and pose for some humorous pictures. He greeted them:

"HELLO THERE, BEATLES. We oughta do some road shows together. We'll get rich."

I n March 1963, while promoting his upcoming fight with Doug Jones, Dad, aka Cassius Marcellus Clay, showed up for a surprise performance at "Poetry Night" at the famous Bitter End club in New York City's Greenwich Village. His poem began:

"Marcellus vanquished Carthage,
Cassius laid Julius Caesar low,
And Clay will flatten Doug Jones
With a mighty, muscled blow."

D espite his prediction of a knockout victory, my father beat Doug Jones on a unanimous decision, never delivering a mighty, muscled blow. He was feeling disappointed at his victory party at Small's Paradise in Harlem, and said candidly,

"I ain't Superman. If the fans think I can do everything I say I can do, then they're crazier than I am."

I love this quote so much I included it in my 2018 memoir, *At Home with Muhammad Ali.*

"GET UP AND FIGHT, SUCKER!"

My father taunted Sonny Liston in their title rematch on May 25, 1965, on a high school hockey rink in Lewiston, Maine, after Liston was knocked out only one minute, 52 seconds into the first round. He yelled at the former champion to get up because he worried everyone would think the fight was fixed, as most people didn't see the knockout punch. When skeptics called it a "phantom punch," Dad insisted it was an "anchor punch" taught to him by movie actor Stepin Fetchit, who had learned it from heavyweight champ Jack Johnson. Videos backed him up, clearly showing that Dad landed a short but powerful twisting right to the jaw as Liston was moving forward.

"**Part of Muhammad's greatness was his ability to be different things to different people.**"

—KAREEM ABDUL-JABBAR

"From the standpoint of his ability to perform and his ability to be involved with the world, Ali was the most important sports figure in history."

—JIM BROWN

HE WAS MY HERO. HE ALWAYS WILL BE."

—SERENA WILLIAMS

HE CARES ABOUT EVERY SINGLE PERSON ON THIS PLANET."

—RALPH BOSTON

"The man who will whup me will be fast, strong, and hasn't been born yet."

My father said this to a reporter after winning the world title on February 25, 1964, when he was asked how long he expected to wear the championship belt.

"I AM AMERICA.

I am the part you won't recognize. But get used to me. Black, confident, cocky; my name, not yours; my religion, not yours; my goals, my own; get used to me."

My father said these inspiring words in 1970 so that all people of all ages would take pride in their identity and be true to who they were, as he was. This quote had a profound influence on many African Americans, from basketball star Lew Alcindor, who would change his name to Kareem Abdul-Jabbar in 1971, to future president Barack Obama, who recited it while paying tribute to my father after he passed in June 2016.

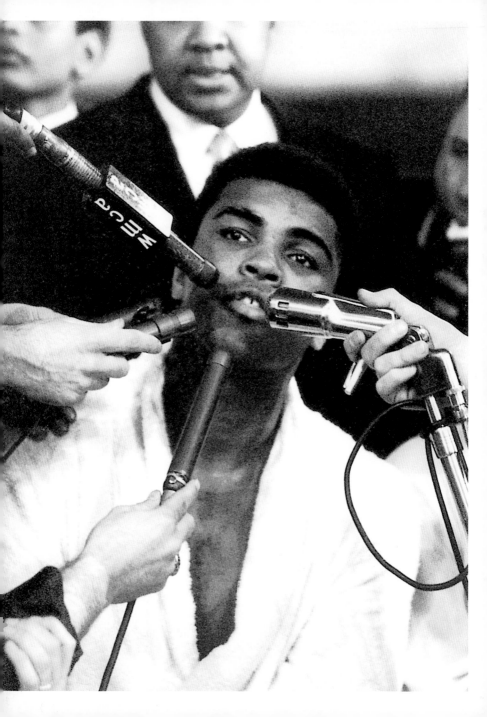

My father always had a fondness for Howard Cosell. He was the first network broadcaster to call him Muhammad Ali. Cosell had also sided with Dad when his heavyweight title was stripped and he was banned from boxing for refusing induction into the armed forces. They appeared together numerous times on *ABC's Wide World of Sports*, often analyzing his fights. Over the years, they came across as a comedy team, with the pompous broadcaster—whose toupee made Dad laugh—being the butt of some of his most memorable one-liners:

"Cosell, you're a phony, and that thing on your head comes from the tail of a pony."

"If I had a lower IQ, I could enjoy your interview."

"Howard, every time you open your mouth, you should be arrested for air pollution."

"You're always talking about, 'Muhammad, you're not the same man you were ten years ago.' Well, I asked your wife, and she told me you're not the same man you was two years ago!"

After Cosell passed away on April 23, 1995, Dad said,

"I have been interviewed by many people, but I enjoyed interviews with Howard the best."

FIGHT II...THE BIG FIGHT EVERYONE IS WAITING TO SEE

MADISON SQ. GARDEN | MON. JAN. 28th

MAIN EVENT - 12 ROUNDS

JOE FRAZIER

> # "I hated every minute of training. But I said, 'DON'T QUIT. Suffer now, and live the rest of your life as a champion.'"

My father disliked training—particularly running two miles early in the morning prior to matches—but he realized it gave him an advantage over opponents when they were both exhausted and victory was on the line. He appreciated and complained about all he endured to become champion—and his words are used as inspiration for countless endeavors requiring practice or study, from sports, to singing and acting, to working. His words have popped up on bulletin boards, websites, and T-shirts. As my father said many times,

"What counts in the ring is what you can do after you're exhausted. The fight is won or lost far away from witnesses—behind the lines, in the gym, and out there on the road, long before I dance under those lights."

"Silence is golden when you can't think of an answer."

One of his most popular sayings, it was shared by my father with countless friends, reporters, and TV hosts throughout his life. Ironically, his "golden rule" didn't really apply to him, because he *always* had an answer.

Dad and me in Los Angeles, 1977

"Sure, I know I got it made while the masses of black people are catchin' hell, but as long as they ain't free, I ain't free."

My father's deep concern for his people never waned, as was confirmed in a 1975 interview with *Playboy*. But over time, he spoke increasingly about his concerns for all people and took every opportunity to bring awareness to the universal human condition.

"Impossible is just a big word thrown around by small men who find it easier to live in the world they've been given than to explore the power they have to change it. Impossible is not a fact. It's an opinion. Impossible is not a declaration. It's a dare. Impossible is potential. Impossible is temporary. **IMPOSSIBLE IS NOTHING.**"

My father knew he would have accomplished little if he was discouraged by people who insisted that what he wanted to do was impossible, both in the ring and in life. These inspirational words were part of the speech on this subject that he delivered in the 1960s at Muslim gatherings and on his college tour. In 2004, Adidas used my father's words and images in its prize-winning "Impossible Is Nothing" marketing campaign.

"THERE'S NOT A MAN ALIVE WHO CAN WHUP ME.

I'm too fast. I'm too smart. I'm too pretty. I should be a postage stamp. That's the only way I'll ever get licked."

As his March 8, 1971, title fight at Madison Square Garden with heavyweight champion Joe Frazier drew near, Dad made a compelling case for why he would win the "Fight of the Century" and stay undefeated. His intention was to intimidate Frazier, but his boastful words also reinforced his own confidence.

In 1985 my father opened one of his fan letters from England and called the telephone number at the bottom of the page. He invited Russ Routledge, a complete stranger, to stay in our home for a two-week visit in Los Angeles. Russ documented his trip with video footage, some of which was featured in Clare Lewins's 2014 documentary, *I Am Ali*. Russ asked my father if there was ever any animosity between him and the men he fought in the ring. Dad looked at him and said,

"No, we're all friends. We only fought for the money."

Dad with Joe Frazier and Floyd Patterson

"Education is the greatest thing."

Dad made this statement on the *Barbara Walters Special* on May 30, 1978, when the host asked him if he'd want his son to be a boxer. He was asked this question many times. He once said that first he'd do everything in his power to try and talk him out of it, then he'd do everything in his power to help him. Only it wasn't his son but his daughter—my sister Laila—who became a boxer!

Dad with me and my younger sister, Laila

"If the measure of greatness is to gladden the heart of every human being on the face of the earth, then he truly was the greatest. In every way he was the bravest, the kindest, and the most excellent of men."

—BOB DYLAN

He belonged to everyone. That means that his impact recognizes no continent, no language, no color, no ocean."

—MAYA ANGELOU

YOUR COURAGE AND DETERMINATION HAVE MADE YOU AN OUTSTANDING CHAMPION."

—NELSON MANDELA

"I wanted America to be America."

My father truly loved America and refused to move to Canada when he was threatened with imprisonment for refusing to be inducted into the US Army. He wanted America to be the just, tolerant, idealistic, and freedom-and-peace-loving country that its name represented to the world. When he said these simple but powerful words to his biographer Thomas Hauser, he was explaining that his stance against the Vietnam War wasn't about trying to be a leader or hero—he was simply acting according to his conscience and felt he was representing all races. He used the same phrase when recalling the great disappointment he felt over being treated like a second-class citizen in Louisville despite having won an Olympic gold medal for his country in 1960. This quote certainly resonates today.

Dad predicted he'd knock out Henry Cooper in the fifth round of their first bout in London on June 18, 1963. After he was almost knocked out himself at the end of the fourth round, he was able to get off the canvas and make good on his prediction with a fifth-round TKO. He later boasted,

"I'M NOT THE GREATEST. I'M THE DOUBLE GREATEST.

Not only do I knock 'em out, I pick the round. I'm the boldest, the prettiest, the most superior, most scientific, most skillfullest fighter in the ring today."

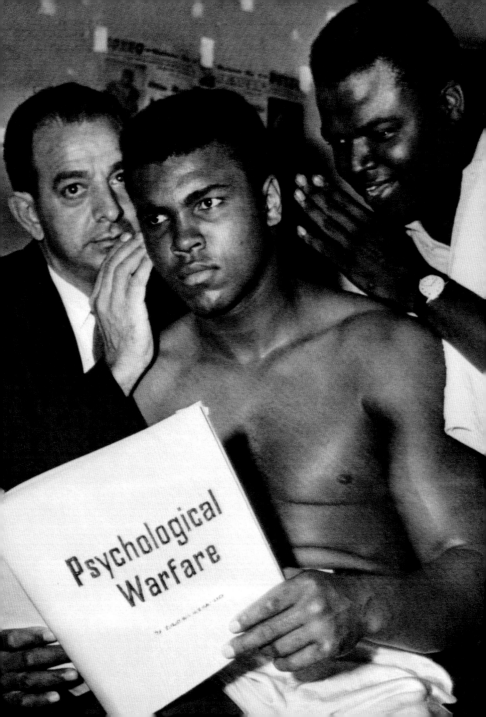

"ALI WILL RETURN. MY GHOST WILL HAUNT ALL ARENAS."

My father said these prophetic words on April 26, 1967, at a coffee shop in Chicago when speaking to journalists Robert Lipsyte and Nicholas von Hoffman two days before refusing military induction in Houston, Texas. He knew that in addition to being sentenced to five years in prison, he'd be stripped of his heavyweight crown and banned from boxing.

"Islam is not a killer religion, **ISLAM MEANS PEACE.** I couldn't just sit home and watch people label Muslims as the reason for this problem."

I n the aftermath of the September 11, 2001, attacks on the World Trade Center and the Pentagon, when many shortsighted individuals jumped to the wrong conclusion that all Muslims were terrorists and were united behind those who attacked this country, my father refused to stay silent. He couldn't bear to see the religion he loved so tragically misrepresented.

114

"It's not the action that makes a thing right or wrong, but the purpose behind the action."

My dad may have said this before I was born in 1976, and he did say it on a *Barbara Walters Special* in 1978, by which time my sister Laila was born, but it's something he always repeated to us when we were growing up.

A train ride with my father, 1976

My father spoke at about 200 colleges during his exile from boxing in the late 1960s. He had six speeches to choose from. These are a few lovely lines from one of his favorites:

"Rivers, lakes, and streams all have different names but they all contain water. Just as religions have different names and they all contain truth, expressed in different ways, forms, and times."

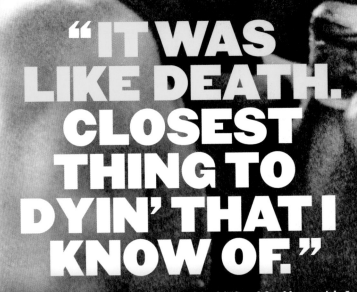

"IT WAS LIKE DEATH. CLOSEST THING TO DYIN' THAT I KNOW OF."

This is how my father summed up his third and final bout with Joe Frazier, the grueling title fight known as the "Thrilla in Manila," on October 1, 1975. After the two gladiators exchanged powerful blows for fourteen rounds in the scorching heat, Frazier chose not to come out for the final round. Dad remembered that the first person he expressed this sentiment to was his longtime trainer, Angelo Dundee, immediately after he was declared the victor.

"People will forget what you said, and they will forget what you did, but they will never forget how you made them feel. I will never look down on the people who look up to me."

I
n late 1978, my father said these words—the first line has been attributed to Carl W. Buehner, Maya Angelou, and others; the second line is his—while dining with our family friend Tim Shanahan, a medical instruments salesman who also lived in Chicago and worked for a charity that arranged for pro athletes to speak to underprivileged kids. Dad was explaining why he signed autographs at restaurants and other public places at the expense of his privacy and time. Years later, Tim shared what was said in his 2016 memoir, *Running with the Champ.*

"THAT ALL YOU GOT, GEORGE?"

George Foreman thought my father was ready to be knocked out after taking so many hard blows for the first seven rounds of their "Rumble in the Jungle" fight on October 30, 1974. After hitting Dad with everything he had, George was startled to hear my father whisper those words in his ear. As George revealed in the documentary *I Am Ali*, he thought, "Yep, that's about it," before he was knocked out in the eighth round.

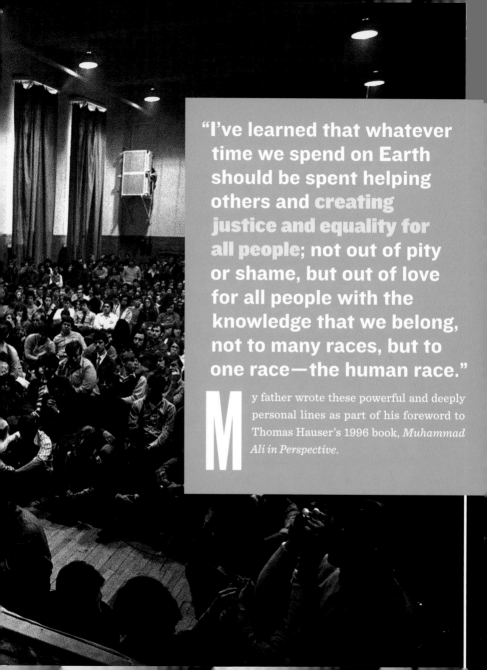

"I've learned that whatever time we spend on Earth should be spent helping others and creating justice and equality for all people; not out of pity or shame, but out of love for all people with the knowledge that we belong, not to many races, but to one race—the human race."

My father wrote these powerful and deeply personal lines as part of his foreword to Thomas Hauser's 1996 book, *Muhammad Ali in Perspective.*

"MUHAMMAD ALI TAUGHT US ALL THAT, WHATEVER COLOR YOU ARE, WHATEVER RELIGION YOU ARE, YOU CAN BE PROUD OF WHO YOU ARE."

—BILL CLINTON

"The man we celebrate today was not just a boxer, or a poet, or an agitator, or a man of peace. He was not just a Muslim, or a black man, or a Louisville kid. He wasn't even just 'The Greatest of All Time.' He was Muhammad Ali, a whole greater than the sum of its parts. He was bigger, brighter, more original and influential than just about anyone of his era. You couldn't have made him up. And yes, he was pretty, too."

—BARACK OBAMA

"ME? WHEEE!"

After a lecture at Harvard during the time he was banned from boxing, my father recited what he proudly declared was the new record holder for shortest poem ever. He said this rhyme often, but it can be traced back to at least August 1963, when he recorded his album, *I Am the Greatest!* He joked to the 200 people in the studio audience at Columbia Records's 30th Street Studios in New York City that he wrote this short poem while he was speaking to them, and that it reflected how it felt to be him. But he didn't tell them that his poem had another meaning: "Me, we"—an expression of community and togetherness.

"I HAVE NOTHING BAD TO SAY ABOUT JOE FRAZIER.

Without him, I wouldn't be who I am and without me, he couldn't be who he is. We've been a pretty good team for four, five years."

My father loved to brag and boast before fights, but he was always gracious and respectful of his defeated opponents. This was demonstrated at a postfight news conference after their third fight in the Philippines, on October 1, 1975. Their rivalry was unparalleled in the 1970s, and their incredible matches became part of boxing lore.

"It is the heart that makes a man great—his intentions, his thoughts, and his convictions."

While my father expressed this concept many times and in many ways over the years, these words were original to our 2004 book, *The Soul of a Butterfly*. They are unique in that he meant them as a response to himself if he were a reporter asking Muhammad Ali about the secret to his success.

Laila with the babysitter, me with Dad, 1978

"If I hated, I couldn't think.
If I hated, I couldn't eat.
If I hated, I couldn't work.
I'd be frustrated. I don't hate."

My father wrote this in *Healing*, a 1996 book he did with Thomas Hauser, but it was a statement he made many times over the course of his life.

Dad at Fighter's Heaven

My father drew inspiration for creating his multifaceted public persona from his father, musicians, poets, TV evangelists, boxer Sugar Ray Robinson, and wrestler Gorgeous George. He often said that it was never him alone who was responsible for his success—that it was God working through him. But he also felt self-made, as he explained to sportswriter Huston Horn for the September 25, 1961, issue of *Sports Illustrated*:

"WHO MADE ME IS ME."

"I done **WRESTLED** with an alligator, I done **TUSSLED** with a whale; **HANDCUFFED** lightning, **THROWN** thunder in jail; only last week, I **MURDERED** a rock, **INJURED** a stone, **HOSPITALIZED** a brick; **I'M SO MEAN I MAKE MEDICINE SICK.**"

Almost every boxing writer said that unbeaten heavyweight champion George Foreman was too tough and mean for my father to have a chance against him, but during the buildup to their fight on October 30, 1974, in Kinshasa, Zaire, Dad said, in an amusing way, that he was even tougher and meaner than the champ. These words would be set to music in his 1976 children's album, *The Adventures of Ali and His Gang vs. Mr. Tooth Decay.*

Before the "Rumble in the Jungle" on October 30, 1974, my father tried to agitate the undefeated heavyweight champion George Foreman by calling him "The Mummy" and insisting he'd beaten only mediocre opponents. Since everyone else was praising Foreman's punching power, Dad seized the opportunity to mock his boxing ability. He resurrected a witty remark he'd used on Sonny Liston in 1963:

"I'VE SEEN GEORGE FOREMAN SHADOWBOXING AND THE SHADOW WON."

"HE WHO IS NOT COURAGEOUS ENOUGH TO TAKE A RISK WILL ACCOMPLISH NOTHING IN LIFE."

When my father said these famous words on a *Barbara Walters Special* in 1978, he was referring to his refusal to be inducted into the army a decade before. "I've taken a lot of risks," he added. Dad also said it, most memorably, to Michael Parkinson during his fourth and final appearance on *Parkinson*, on his birthday, January 17, 1981, when the famed British interviewer tried to deter him from fighting one last time.

"I'll tell you how I'd *like* to be remembered: as a black man who won the heavyweight title and who was humorous and who treated everyone right. As a man who never looked down on those who looked up to him and who helped as many of his people as he could—financially and also in their FIGHT FOR FREEDOM, JUSTICE, AND EQUALITY."

My father said this in a featured interview in *Playboy* magazine that was published in November 1975.

"God tests me every day that I wake up with my disease, and I pass the test every time."

When my father was living with Parkinson's, he had challenging days, but he remained spiritually and emotionally strong. He reflected on his condition to Tim Shanahan, who years later included these words in his 2016 memoir of their friendship, *Running with the Champ.*

My father recited his stirring poem "The Recipe to Life" so many times that he knew it by heart. However, he is perhaps best remembered reciting it during a broadcast on British television on September 16, 1974. Sitting in a ring in street clothes six weeks before he'd take the heavyweight title from George Foreman, he responded to British interviewer David Frost's question about how he'd like to be remembered:

"He took a few cups of **LOVE**.

He took one tablespoon of **PATIENCE**,

One teaspoon of **GENEROSITY**.

One pint of **KINDNESS**.

He took one quart of **LAUGHTER**,

One pinch of **CONCERN**.

And then he mixed **WILLINGNESS**
with **HAPPINESS**,

He added lots of **FAITH**,

And he stirred it up well.

Then he spread it over a span
of a lifetime.

And he served it to each and every
deserving person he met."

MUHAMMAD ALI:

1942

JAN. 17 — Cassius Marcellus Clay Jr. is born in Louisville, Kentucky.

1954

At the age of 12, Cassius Clay starts boxing.

1959

Clay wins the National AAU Light Heavyweight Championship.

1960

Clay wins his second National AAU Light Heavyweight Championship.

SEPT. 5 — At the 1960 Rome Olympic Games, Clay defeats Zbigniew Pietrzykowski of Poland to win the light heavyweight boxing gold medal.

OCT. 29 — Clay wins his first professional fight on a six-round decision over Tunney Hunsaker in Louisville.

1962

FEB. 10 — Clay is knocked down for the first time as a professional but wins his eleventh consecutive match with a fourth-round TKO over Sonny Banks in his first match in New York City.

NOV. 15 — Clay defeats his first significant fighter, Archie Moore, with a fourth-round TKO, as he had predicted.

1963

JUNE 18 — In London, in his first pro bout outside the US, Clay is almost knocked out in the fourth round but, as he predicted, knocks out Henry Cooper in the fifth round, earning him a heavyweight title.

1964

FEB. 25 — At 22, Clay defeats heavily favored champion Sonny Liston to win the world heavyweight boxing crown in Miami.

FEB. 25 — Clay announces he has converted from Baptist to the Nation of Islam.

MARCH 6 — Clay, now Cassius X, officially changes his name to Muhammad Ali.

AUG. 14 — Ali marries Sonji Roi.

1965

MAY 25 — On what some will call "the phantom punch," Ali knocks out Sonny Liston in the first round of their title rematch in Lewiston, Maine.

A TIMELINE

NOV. 22 Angered that former heavyweight champion Floyd Patterson continues to call him by his slave name, Ali dominates the challenger before scoring a twelfth-round TKO in Las Vegas.

1966

NOV. 14 Ali culminates a year in which he has already defended his title against George Chuvalo, Henry Cooper, Brian London, and Karl Mildenberger with a third-round TKO over Cleveland Williams in Houston, in what many will say was his greatest performance.

1967

FEB. 6 Ali defeats Ernie Terrell in Houston to unify the heavyweight crown.

MARCH 22 Ali knocks out Zora Folley in the seventh round in New York City, his ninth successful title defense. It will be his last fight for three and a half years.

APRIL 28 In Houston, Ali refuses to join the US Army, citing his opposition to the Vietnam War. The New York State Athletic Commission and the World Boxing Association strip Ali of his world heavyweight title, and he is banned from boxing.

JUNE 20 Ali is convicted of draft evasion, sentenced to five years in prison, and fined $10,000. He will appeal the sentence, continuing to claim that as a minister of the Nation of Islam he is a conscientious objector opposed to all unholy wars.

AUG. 17 Ali marries Belinda Boyd.

Unable to box in America and with his passport revoked, Ali begins to lecture on college campuses to make a living.

1970

OCT. 26 Ali is allowed to fight in Atlanta and defeats Jerry Quarry with a third-round TKO.

1971

MARCH 8 "The Fight of the Century" takes place between unbeaten "People's Champion" Ali and unbeaten heavyweight champion Joe Frazier in Madison Square Garden. Frazier knocks down Ali and wins by a unanimous decision in fifteen rounds.

APRIL 19 The legal fight under the case name Cassius Marcellus Clay Jr. v. United States is argued before the US Supreme Court.

JUNE 28 The US Supreme Court reverses Ali's 1967 conviction with an 8–0 ruling, confirming that as a minister of the Nation of Islam he is exempt from serving in the army.

JULY 26 Ali wins the vacant **NABF** heavyweight title with a twelfth-round **TKO** of his Louisville childhood friend Jimmy Ellis.

1972

SEPT. 20 Ali wins his eighth consecutive match since losing to Frazier with a seventh-round **TKO** of Floyd Patterson.

1973

MARCH 31 Ali has his jaw broken and is defeated for the second time, losing his **NABF** crown to Ken Norton on a twelve-round decision in San Diego.

SEPT. 10 Ali regains the **NABF** title on a twelve-round decision over Ken Norton in LA.

1974

JAN. 28 Ali and Frazier, who lost his heavyweight title to George Foreman, have a rematch in Madison Square Garden. Ali wins in twelve rounds on a unanimous decision.

Ali and actress and model Veronica Porché begin a relationship. They will marry according to the Islamic tradition at the Presidential Compound in N'Sele, Zaire, and in 1977, in Los Angeles. They will have two daughters, Hana and Laila.

OCT. 30 In the "Rumble in the Jungle" in Kinshasa, Zaire, Ali shocks the world again by knocking out unbeaten George Foreman in the eighth round to regain the world heavyweight title.

1975

OCT. 1 In the "Thrilla in Manila" in the Philippines, Ali defeats Joe Frazier with a fourteenth-round **TKO**. He will call this his greatest fight because of his age, his great opponent, and the extreme heat.

OCT. 1 Ali's autobiography, *The Greatest: My Own Story*, written with Richard Durham, is published.

1976

JUNE 15 Muhammad and Veronica's first daughter, Hana, is born.

SEPT. 28 Ali defends his title by winning close decision over Ken Norton in New York.

1977

The movie of Ali's life, *The Greatest*, in which he plays himself, is released.

DEC. 30 Muhammad and Veronica's second daughter, Laila, is born.

1978

FEB. 15 Ali loses his title to 1976 Olympic champion Leon Spinks in fifteen rounds by a split decision.

SEPT. 15 Ali becomes the first three-time world heavyweight champion with a unanimous fifteen-round decision over Leon Spinks in the Louisiana Superdome. It will be his last victory.

1979

JUNE 27 Ali announces his retirement.

1980

OCT. 2 Hoping to win the heavyweight title for the fourth time, Ali comes out of retirement to face unbeaten heavyweight Larry Holmes in Caesars Palace in Las Vegas. Holmes dominates the fight, and it is stopped in the tenth round—it will be the only time Ali didn't go the distance.

1981

DEC. 11 Ali's career comes to an end, as he loses a ten-round decision to Trevor Berbick in the Bahamas.

1984

Although he had shown signs prior to his comeback in 1980, Ali is diagnosed with Parkinson's disease.

1986

NOV. 19 Ali marries his fourth wife, Yolanda "Lonnie" Williams.

1990

NOV. 29 In Iraq, Ali convinces dictator Saddam Hussein to free fifteen American civilians who were taken hostage in August.

1996

JULY 19 To everyone's surprise and his delight, Ali lights the Olympic flame at the Opening Ceremony for the Atlanta Summer Games.

2001

SEPT. Actor Will Smith, who played him in the movie *Ali*, is at his side when he states that Islam is a religion of peace and that it is wrong for anyone to assume that Muslim Americans have sided with the terrorists who attacked the United States on 9/11.

2005

NOV. 9 Ali is awarded the Presidential Medal of Freedom, the nation's highest civilian award.

2015

DEC. 9 Ali denounces presidential candidates who favor a ban on Muslims entering the United States.

2016

JUNE 3 Ali dies at age 74 in Scottsdale, Arizona.

YEAR	DATE	OPPONENT	LOCATION	RESULT	DECISION
1960	Oct. 29	Tunney Hunsaker	Louisville, KY	W	UD
	Dec. 27	Herbert Siler	Miami, FL	W	TKO
1961	Jan. 17	Anthony Sperti	Miami, FL	W	TKO
	Feb. 7	Jimmy Robinson	Miami, FL	W	KO
	Feb. 21	Donnie Fleeman	Miami, FL	W	RTD
	Apr. 19	Lamar Clark	Louisville, KY	W	KO/
	Jun. 26	Duke Sabwedong	Las Vegas, NV	W	UD /
	Jul. 22	Alonzo Johnson	Louisville, KY	W	UD/
	Oct. 7	Alex Miteff	Louisville, KY	W	TKO
	Nov. 29	Willi Besmanoff	Louisville, KY	W	TKO
1962	Feb. 10	Lucian Banks	New York, NY	W	TKO
	Feb. 28	Jack Wagner	Miami, FL	W	TKO
	Apr. 23	George Logan	Miami, FL	W	TKO
	May 19	Billy Daniels	New York, NY	W	TKO
	Jul. 20	Alejandro Lavorante	Los Angeles, CA	W	KO/
	Nov. 15	Archie Moore	Los Angeles, CA	W	TKO
1963	Jan. 24	Charles Powell	Pittsburgh, PA	W	KO/
	Mar. 13	Doug Jones	New York, NY	W	UD/
	Jun. 18	Henry Cooper	London, UK	W	TKO
1964	Feb. 25	Sonny Liston	Miami, FL	W	RTD
1965	May 25	Sonny Liston	Lewiston, ME	W	KO/
	Nov. 22	Floyd Patterson	Las Vegas, NV	W	TKO
1966	Mar. 29	George Chuvalo	Toronto, Canada	W	UD/
	May 21	Henry Cooper	London, UK	W	TKO
	Aug. 6	Brian London	London, UK	W	KO/
	Sep. 10	Karl Mildenberger	Frankfurt, Germany	W	TKO/
	Nov. 14	Cleveland Williams	Houston, TX	W	TKO
1967	Feb. 6	Ernie Terrell	New York, NY	W	UD/
	Mar. 22	Zora Folley	New York, NY	W	KO/
1970	Oct. 26	Jerry Quarry	Atlanta, GA	W	RTD
	Dec. 7	Oscar Bonavena	New York, NY	W	TKO/

DATE	OPPONENT	LOCATION	RESULT	DECISION/ROUND
Mar. 8	Joe Frazier	New York, NY	L	UD/15
Jul. 26	Jimmy Ellis	Houston, TX	W	TKO/12
Nov. 17	Buster Mathis	Houston, TX	W	UD/12
Dec. 26	Jurgen Blin	Zurich, Switzerland	W	KO/7
Apr. 1	McArthur Foster	Tokyo, Japan	W	UD/15
May 1	George Chuvalo	Vancouver, Canada	W	UD/12
Jun. 27	Jerry Quarry	Las Vegas, NV	W	TKO/7
Jul. 19	Alvin Lewis	Dublin, Ireland	W	TKO/11
Sep. 20	Floyd Patterson	New York, NY	W	RTD/7
Nov. 21	Bob Foster	Stateline, NV	W	KO/8
Feb. 14	Joe Bugner	Las Vegas, NV	W	UD/12
Mar. 31	Ken Norton	San Diego, CA	L	SD/12
Sep. 10	Ken Norton	Inglewood, CA	W	SD/12
Oct. 20	Rudy Lubbers	Jakarta, Indonesia	W	UD/12
Jan. 28	Joe Frazier	New York, NY	W	UD/12
Oct. 30	George Foreman	Kinshasa, Zaire	W	KO/8
Mar. 24	Chuck Wepner	Cleveland, OH	W	TKO/15
May 16	Ron Lyle	Las Vegas, NV	W	TKO/11
Jul. 1	Joe Bugner	Kuala Lumpur, Malaysia	W	UD/15
Oct. 1	Joe Frazier	Quezon, Philippines	W	RTD/14
Feb. 20	Jean Coopman	San Juan, P.R.	W	KO/5
Apr. 30	Jimmy Young	Landover, MD	W	UD/15
May 24	Richard Dunn	Munich, Germany	W	TKO/5
Sep. 28	Ken Norton	New York, NY	W	UD/15
May 16	Alfredo Evangelista	Landover, MD	W	UD/15
Sep. 29	Ernie Shavers	New York, NY	W	UD/15
Feb. 15	Leon Spinks	Las Vegas, NV	L	SD/15
Sep. 15	Leon Spinks	New Orleans, LA	W	UD/15
Oct. 2	Larry Holmes	Las Vegas, NV	L	RTD/11
Dec. 11	Trevor Berbick	Nassau, Bahamas	L	UD/10

ETIRED BETWEEN ROUNDS | UD: UNANIMOUS DECISION | MD: MAJORITY DECISION | TKO: TECHNICAL KNOCKOUT | KO: KNOCKOUT

ACKNOWLEDGMENTS

'd like to thank Danny Peary and my editor, Suzanne Rafer. Without their vision, dedication, and patience, this book would not exist. It was truly a team effort.

And a special thanks to Dustin Bingham, Gene Kilroy, and Danny Cooper, and to my agent, Jill Marr, for all her hard work.

Thank you! My father would be proud.

PHOTO CREDITS